THE 5 THINGS YOU SHOULD KNOW BEFORE PATENTING YOUR INVENTION

MANUEL ALCAYDE DÍAZ

FOREWORD

In this book I narrate what other patent experts don't tell you before patenting your invention, so you don`t invest in a long and expensive process that ends in a result that is very different from what you should expect or what they told you. I will not bore you by giving you theoretical explanations of the Patent Law, this book is practical, handy, direct and explains in a pleasant and easy-to-understand way whether or not it is convenient for you to patent your invention. In less than 30 minutes you will have all the necessary knowledge to decide whether or not to undertake a process that usually takes months or even years of dedication and effort before making a profit.

My professional career of over 29 years in which I have been advising inventors in the field of Industrial Property at an international level; PCT, WIPO, USPTO, CHINA PATENTS AND TRADEMARK OFFICE, EPO, etc., allows me to have the knowledge to solve doubts, concerns and some false beliefs that inventors have about what a patent is and what can be patented, while this experience has also allowed me to explain in a practical and infallible way the most important things that you should know so that you don' t waste your time and money with your invention or, on the contrary, this book will help you to decide to file a patent and take advantage of your ingenuity.

Before explaining the reasons and arguments, let me show you real results published by the World Intellectual Property Organization (WIPO).

The following graph shows the relationship between the number of patents applied and patents granted during 2020 in some of the main countries:

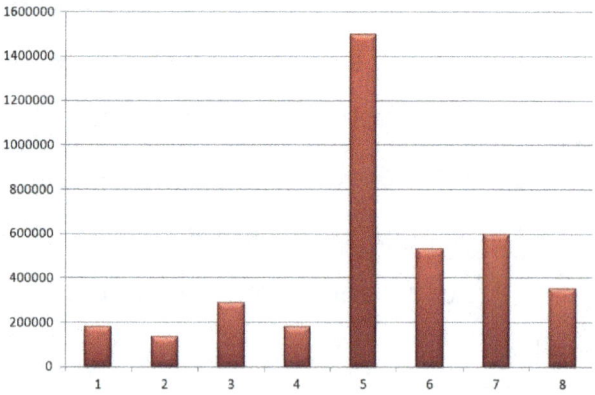

1. PATENTS FILED IN THE EPO
2. PATENTS GRANTED IN THE EPO

3. PATENTS FILED IN JAPAN
4. PATENTS GRANTED IN JAPAN

5. PATENTS FILED IN CHINA
6. PATENTS GRANTED IN CHINA

7. PATENTS FILED IN USA
8. PATENTS GRANTED IN USA

EPO: European Patent Office

Source: *WIPO IP Statistics Data Center.*
https://www3.wipo.int/ipstats/

The first thing that stands out is that just in the Republic of China more patent applications are filed than in the next three patent-producing countries together (despite the fact that we have considered all of Europe as a single bloc).

Another thing that stands out is that it is in China where the percentage of denied patent applications is higher; as you can see only 35% are granted. In the rest of the countries the percentage of granted patents is higher than in China, but **there still are a huge number of patents that are filed and finally denied.**

Taking as an example another random country; Spain, during the year 2020, 1,555 patent applications were filed and only 641 were granted, this means that 59% were denied in proportion to those applications filed in the same year.

In the following graph you can verify this correlation:

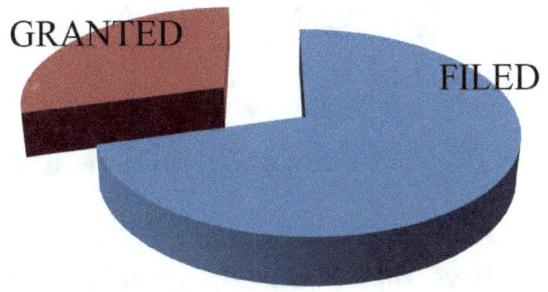

Nextly I will explain everything you need to know in order to acquire some essential know-how that is indispensable before starting your project.

1. EVERY INVENTION MUST HAVE THREE ESSENTIAL REQUIREMENTS:

1. TO BE NEW

2. TO HAVE AN INVENTIVE STEP / NON OBVIOUS

3. TO HAVE INDUSTRIAL APPLICABILITY / USEFUL

1. **The novelty requirement** includes disclosures or exposures that you could have made yourself. Therefore, until the moment the patent is filed, you cannot promote it and you must keep it secret. Currently, patent examiners also check the Internet, Search Engines and Social Networks to verify the novelty of an invention, so you must be very careful.

2. The requisite for **inventive activity** is the Sword of Damocles which jeopardizes the value and also the grant of all inventions. It is understood that an invention has an inventive step when examined by an expert in the specific field, and that this expert is aware of all the patents that exist and all the inventions

published or used in the market, said expert considers that your invention cannot be deduced in an obvious manner.

Both novelty and inventive steps are examined globally. This means that if your invention is not patented in your country or if your invention is not disclosed by any means, but is protected as a patent or utility model in any other country in the world, your invention would not meet the requirement of novelty or the inventive step.

3. **The industrial activity** requirement means that the object or result of your invention must be something that can be manufactured and marketed and must be enabled. Procedures also can be patented as long as they lead to a tangible result, such as; treated water,

medicines, or a procedure that allows the elaboration of a specific product in a more efficient, economical or safe way. Cooking recipes can also be patented as long as they meet the inventive step requirement, that is; that the cooking recipe is not obvious to a cooking expert.

In this regard, and based purely on my experience, I can assure you that the simple combination of ingredients to give rise to a new product does not meet the requirement of inventive steps. To be admitted as a patent, a cooking recipe, a cosmetic product or any other product obtained through a particular process, must have a certain complexity and solve some technical difficulty. For example; some very specific cooking times necessary to a specific result, centrifugation of the product or part of its ingredients, filtering, time to mature, method of collection of the product, specific and essential temperature range, etc.

At this point it is interesting for you to know that there are two different ways to protect your invention, or in other words, there are two types or modalities of patents: Invention Patents and Utility Models.

- **Modality A. The Invention Patent**: It confers the holder the exclusivity or monopoly of the invention for 20 years. In patents, it is mandatory to request a report called the State of the Art Report (SOAR) which examines the novelty and inventive activity of your invention **worldwide** and also is necessary to make a mandatory exam called the Substantive Examination, which assesses the result of the SOAR and is based on it. This exam grants or denies your patent. The amount of both rates are high but if you are self-employed or a company you could probably get some grant for the internationalization of your invention.

The greatest advantage of protecting an invention under the patent modality is that once it is granted, the government guarantees that there is no other invention equal or similar to yours. This means that you can invest in the manufacture and sale of the product of your invention without any concern about competitors, also you can sell or license your patent for a high amount because you can guarantee the potential buyer that your product is an **exclusive and inimitable product.**

- **Modality B. The Utility Model:**

This type of patent only exists in some countries, specifically: Germany, Argentina, Armenia, Australia, Austria, ARIPO, Belarus, Belgium, Brazil, Bulgaria, China, Chile, Colombia, Costa Rica, Denmark, Slovakia, Spain, Estonia, Ethiopia, Russian Federation, Philippines, Finland, France, Georgia , Greece, Guatemala, Hungary, Ireland, Italy, Japan, Kazakhstan, Kenya, Kyrgyzstan, Malaysia, Mexico, OAPI, Netherlands, Peru, Poland, Portugal, Czech Republic, Republic of Korea, Republic of Moldova, Tajikistan, Trinidad and Tobago , Turkey, Ukraine, Uruguay and Uzbekistan.The utility model also confers on its holder the exclusivity or monopoly of their invention, but the duration is 10 years. Besides the utility model is only allowed in some countries, if an invention is already protected as a utility model in any country, it is enough requirement for any other patent not to meet the novelty or inventive step requirement.

The biggest difference between both modalities is that, based on the Law of Patents, the utility model is not required to report on the novelty and inventive activity of your invention, therefore the State of the Art Report (SOAR) is not required. The Substantive Examination is not required either. Therefore, if you protect your invention as a utility model, you have the **advantages** that it will be much **cheaper** and you will have it

granted in a shorter time than if you protect your invention as an invention patent.

But you have the **drawback** that despite the fact that the protection of your invention is granted and guaranteed by the government; you cannot know if there is an exact or a similar invention patented before yours, so **it is difficult to find a manufacturing partner, sell or license your utility model**. Take into account that for a third party to commit to manufacturing your invention or that this third party wants to buy your utility model or obtain a license for it, he or she will ask you for the guarantee that it is a unique and exclusive product. Obviously the Utility Model cannot provide that guarantee. For all these reasons, the protection of an invention under the Utility Model modality is more advisable when you have the purpose of manufacturing and selling the product resulting from your invention by yourself.

On the other hand, keep in mind that if a third party has knowledge in the field of patents or is well advised by an expert in Industrial Property and he or she is interested in manufacturing or selling the object of your invention; he or she could file a judicial appeal alleging that your invention lacks novelty or inventive step. If this happens, that subject would be obliged to request the State of the Art Report (SOAR) from the Patent and Trademark Office, leaving the protection and value of your invention subject to the result of said report.

Taking into account everything I have explained and despite this inconvenience; You may be interested in protecting your invention as a utility model because as long as it is not proven in court that it is not new and that it does not have an inventive step, since you are the owner of the utility model you are entitled to continue manufacturing and selling the invention exclusively until finishing the judicial process, which may take more than a year from the first notification you receive.

For all these reasons, depending on your circumstances, you may be interested in protecting your invention as a patent or as a utility model.

2. IDEAS IN THEMSELVES ARE NOT PATENTABLE.

Every invention must have a technical component in order to be patented. If your idea contains technical procedures, or mechanisms, or necessary gadgets to achieve this idea, it could be patented, but it should be very clear to you that you are not patenting the idea itself, rather you are patenting the manner or mechanisms by which you manage to carry your idea out.

This means that if the same idea or the same solution to a technical problem can be achieved using different procedures, or different gadgets or mechanisms, each of said procedures or gadgets can be a different patent.

The essential condition is that each procedure or gadget must have an inventive step with respect to the other procedures or devices, or in other words, each one of the subsequent inventions cannot be deduced in an obvious way from the former inventions.

It is very frequent that splendid ideas do not have a material support or an innovative technical support for the development or implementation of said idea, reason for which it cannot be patented.

Throughout my professional life there have been many clients who have transmitted fantastic ideas to me, but they lacked a technical procedure, a mechanism or a gadget. Or even thought this idea had a technical procedure, a mechanism or a gadget; those had no novelty or inventive activity; hence they were not patentable ideas.

Nextly, I will expose two real examples of some clients of mine who had great ideas but for the reason explained, these ideas could not be patented.

- **First Example**: Suitcase with GPS.

Somethihg that happens very frequently is that when somebody arrives at the destination airport, the suitcase has not arrived on the same flight as theirs or that the suitcase has been sent to another airport, we do not get any answers of the localization of the suitcase and it takes days or even weeks to find it. To avoid this problem, a good solution could be to incorporate a GPS in any part of the suitcase, so that if the suitcase does not arrive at their destination, knowing where it is, the airport staff can send it to them on the next flight.

This looks like an excellent solution to a problem and you can apply for a great patent! But unfortunately both the suitcase and the GPS are already invented and unless you can provide a novel procedure or a novel mechanism in order to incorporate the GPS into the suitcase, this idea could not be accepted as a patent. . On the other hand; If there is a technique or a mechanism to incorporate the GPS into the suitcase which provides usefulness and advantages in said process of coupling or inserting the GPS into the suitcase, the entire set could be patented.

Be careful! Remember that what is patented is the mechanism or process to achieve the idea (a GPS incorporated in the suitcase), but not the idea itself. That is to say, that if another person invents a mechanism to incorporate the GPS in the suitcase that is different and that is not obviously deduced from the previous one; such a mechanism, it can also be protected as another different patent for the same idea.

- **Second example**: Casinos and Games of Chance.

In some East Asian countries, gambling and casinos are prohibited, which is why many inhabitants of these countries travel abroad to carry out these activities.

One of our clients presented us with a great idea so that the inhabitants of those countries could play and carry out the same activities as in a casino without having to travel to their countries. His idea consisted of installing bingo, roulette and other games of chance in passenger planes to be able to play once the plane is in full flight within an international zone which is a type of extraterritory governed by international law and not by a particular country´s Law. As you may have already learned the brilliant idea of the client lacked a technical aspect, that is, a process or a mechanism that provides a technological advantage.

In this case, the proposed idea could only be patented if the client who had the idea also provided a process for adapting the airplane cabin to the gambling facility; or the mechanisms for coupling to the aircraft cabin or any other part or mechanism that incorporates a certain advantage to achieve that end and of course always fulfilling the requirements of being new and that cannot be clearly deduced from what is already invented, (inventive step). As you have already learned; what really constitutes the patent or the utility model and can be protected, are those mechanisms but not the idea itself.

3. PROHIBITIONS OF THE PATENT LAW ON NON-PATENTABLE INVENTIONS OR CREATIONS.

At this point, to dispel any doubt, I consider it useful for you to know everything that, by Law, you cannot consider obtaining an economic right based on a patent. In this regard, the Law is basically the same for all countries, so that the following list of elements that are not patentable is applicable to most countries:

1.-

a) *Discoveries, scientific theories and mathematical methods.*

b) *Literary, artistic or any other aesthetic creation, as well as scientific works.*

c) *The plans, rules and methods for the exercise of intellectual activities, for games or for economic-commercial activities, as well as computer programs. (With the exception of some countries such as the USA, where computer programs are allowed to be patented).*

d) *The ways of presenting information.*

The provisions of the previous section exclude the patentability of the materials or activities mentioned therein only to the extent that the patent application or patent refers exclusively to one of them considered as such.

2. Inventions whose commercial exploitation is contrary to public order or ethical customs, without being able to consider the exploitation of an invention as such for the mere fact that it is prohibited by a legal or regulatory provision.

In particular, the following shall not be considered patentable under the provisions of the preceding paragraph:

a) Human cloning procedures.

b) The procedures for modifying the germinal genetic identity of the human being.

c) The use of human embryos for industrial or commercial purposes.

d) The procedures for modifying the genetic identity of the animals that entail for these sufferings without substantial medical or veterinary utility for man or the animal, and the animals resulting from such procedures.

2.- Plant varieties and animal breeds. However, inventions that have plants or animals as their object will be patentable if the technical feasibility of the invention is not limited to a specific plant variety or animal breed.

3.- The essentially biological procedures for obtaining plants or animals. For these purposes, those procedures that consist entirely of natural phenomena such as crossing or selection, will be considered essentially biological.

The provisions of the preceding paragraph shall not affect the patentability of inventions whose object is a microbiological procedure or any other technical procedure or a product obtained by said procedures.

4. The human body, in the different stages of its constitution and development, as well as the simple discovery of one of its elements, including the sequence or partial sequence of a gene.

However, an element isolated from the human body or otherwise obtained by a technical procedure, including the total or partial sequence of a gene, may be considered as a patentable invention, even if the structure of said element is identical to that of a natural element.

The industrial application of a total or partial sequence of a gene must be explicitly stated in the patent application.

4. THE CASE OF COMPUTER PROGRAMS AND APPs.

As indicated above in section 1.C, in some countries The Law explicitly prohibits the protection of computer programs as a patent. This also includes APPs, therefore all types of software and computer programming.

You could only protect an invention that works based on software, when the rest of the elements that make up the invention contribute to that invention as a whole, and all these elements have novelty and inventive activity, but the software itself is not protected.

Nextly, I will give you a real example of a patented and granted invention; a handcart adapted for the collection of wild fruits and berries. This trolley has the particularity that it always maintains the correct horizontal attitude no matter how steep the ground may be, this occurs due to a software that calculates the degree of inclination at any time and sends an order to each of the four legs with the wheels at their ends, despite that without this software the invention would not work, the patent does not protect this computer program nor does it protect the idea itself, what the patent protects is the way in which said software is executed, providing the desired result; that is, the entire set of elements and their configuration; the type of legs that make up the cart, its connections with the tray where the berries are deposited, where and how the electronic components are located and the set of elements and their configuration in such a way that they make it work satisfactorily, fulfilling its purpose efficiently .

Taking advantage of this example, we are going to re-emphasize that controversial concept of **inventive activity**:

In our example, if a third party were to develop the same idea with the same objective, even using the same or similar software, that is, another person or company that manufacture another cart for collecting wild fruits that works through software, but this new trolley has a different configuration, different characteristics of the parts or elements that make up the trolley, and that trolley obtains a result equal to or better than the previous trolley; it would be patentable as long as it is new and **cannot be deduced in an obvious way** from the previous invention.

As you have already learned, in the case of utility models, novelty and inventiveness are not examined, so if the utility model has industrial application it is granted. In this case, the prior patent or model could challenge the validity of the utility model despite having been granted.

Computer programs and APPs cannot be protected as patents in most countries, for example, they cannot be protected in any of the countries of the European Community nor in China. In contrast, computer programs can be protected as patents in the US.

5. NON-PATENTABLE CREATIONS MAY HAVE COPYRIGHT.

Despite the fact that you cannot obtain economic profitability because it was not possible to patent your idea, you can obtain moral recognition that you are the inventor or creator of the idea.

As we have already seen, it is very common to have a good idea but if it lacks a technological component, it cannot be protected as a patent. Using as an example those already mentioned: The idea of GPS in the suitcase, casinos installed on planes, or other inventions, or mentioning other examples; a business model or a business organization system that is new and has an inventive step but is lacking in an industrial application since a final physical object cannot be manufactured.

Let's give you one more example; the firms that take a pizza to your home; the case of DOMINO'S PIZZA OR TELEPIZZA.

Despite the fact that today it is something very common, at the beginning of the 70s it was a most avant-garde idea, a business as simple as cooking food and taking it to your home did not exist, it was a great idea and a fantastic business model, but the lack of a technical procedure nor a technical mechanizing, hence, it was not possible to obtain a patent for that idea, therefore many companies have copied this idea so they take cooked food to your home.

In all these cases where you develop a business model, a business organization system, a way of presenting information or that you simply have a great idea that cannot be patented, you can just get a moral right over that idea, for this you need to embody it in written support, either paper or electronic support and submit it to the Intellectual Property Registry.

The CopyRight acknowledges that you are the author of that idea and that it is not any other person or company, but it does not give you the exclusive right to carry out the idea, that is, any other person or company can develop or put it into practice without your consent. In the case that your idea or invention is not patentable, another option would be to try to sell your idea in a book, write about it and if it is successful, you would have an economic benefit from the sales.

Finally in this book, I am going to show you a real example of a patent which is called: "Folding table with two-position leg lock" requested in 2016.

As you can see, every patent has three main blocks:

1. Memory

2. Figures or drawings

3. The claims. The claims are the most important part of a patent because in them you have to explain the technical characteristics of your invention that have novelty and inventive activity without alluding to qualities or advantages of your invention. The claims have to be strictly technical properties of your invention.

4. The summary

Abstract

A folding table has a pair of regular, non-foldable legs (104) and a pair of foldable legs (106) that move between a use configuration and a storage configuration. The foldable legs (106) incorporate a two-position lock mechanism (122) allows the legs to be locked in either the use configuration where the legs cooperatively support the table top (102) or the storage configuration where the legs are positioned parallel to the table top (102). The table top (102) includes a notched lip (126) that allows the legs to lie substantially flush against the table top (102).

Description

Folding Table with Two-Position Leg Lock

BACKGROUND

Folding tables are commonly used where temporary entertainment or work surfaces are needed. Conventional folding tables generally stand on multiple legs, and the legs rotate 90 degrees for storage. Such conventional designs are suitable when *the at least one dimension (e.g., length, width, or diameter) of table top is greater than the length of the legs. For example, in many conventional folding tables, each leg individually folds up along one side of the table top and does not extend beyond the size of the table top surface. The hallmarks of such conventional 90 degree leg rotation designs are simplicity and set-up speed.*

High top folding tables, such as folding cocktail tables, present unique design challenges because the folding legs are often longer than any dimension of the table top and, thus, require additional storage space. As the length of the legs increase, stability becomes a concern, forcing designers to look beyond the simple 90 degree leg rotation designs common in conventional folding tables for alternatives that allow fast and easy set-up, compact storage, and stability. It is with these considerations in mind that the present invention was conceived. BRIEF SUMMARY

The following summary discusses various aspects of the invention described more fully in the detailed description and claimed herein. It i s not intended and should not be used to limit the claimed invention to only such aspects or to require the invention to include all such aspects.

A folding table with a two position leg lock is described herein and illustrated in the accompanying figures. Aspects of the folding table include an upper support member, such as a table top or frame, a pair of regular (i.e., non-foldable) legs, and a pair of foldable legs. The regular legs and the foldable legs are configured to cooperatively support the table top in a substantially horizontal orientation in a use configuration. In various embodiments, the folding table includes a pair of notches defined by the lip of the table top. The notches allow the legs to lie substantially flush with the bottom of the lip and provide a generally flat profile while in the storage configuration.

The foldable legs include a base leg portion that is pivotally connected to one of the leg extensions by foldable leg connectors. In operation, the base leg portions and the extensions pivot about the connectors moving from the use configuration where lower ends of the base leg portions point in the opposite direction from the upper ends of the leg extensions to a storage configuration where the lower ends of the base leg portions point in the same direction as the upper ends of the leg extensions.

A lock mechanism allows the foldable legs and the extensions to be selectively fixed in the use configuration or the storage configuration. Aspects of the two position lock mechanism include, by way of example, a lock pin main connector extending from one of the leg extensions. The lock pin is biased to normally extend beyond the outside edge of the leg extension toward the base leg member. An actuator or handle allows an operator to apply a force opposing the bias to *retract the lock pin thereby disengaging the lock mechanism.*

A use receptacle and a storage receptacle configured to operatively receive the lock pin are defined by the base leg segment. The lock pin and the receptacles lie on the circumference of a circle with a radius, r, and centered on the foldable leg connector. When in the use configuration, the lock pin and the use receptacle are aligned. And, when in the storage configuration, the lock pin and the storage receptacle are aligned. When the lock pin is operatively engaged with one of the receptacles, the relative positions of the base leg segment and the leg extension become fixed. Because they are connected together and the positions of the their upper ends are locked by the attachment to the table top, the regular legs and the foldable legs cannot move relative to one another, the folding table is locked in the current configuration until released.

BRIEF DESCRIPTION OF THE DRAWINGS

Further features, aspects, and advantages of the present disclosure will become better understood by reference to the following figures, wherein elements are not to scale so as to more clearly show the details and wherein like reference numbers indicate like elements throughout the several views:

FIG. 1 is a perspective view of one embodiment of the folding table in a use configuration; FIG. 2 is a bottom plan view of one embodiment of the folding table in a storage configuration;

FIG. 3A is a simplified sectional side elevation view of one embodiment of the folding table in the use configuration, taken along section line 3-3;

FIG. 3B is a simplified sectional side elevation view showing the folding table from FIG. 3A in an intermediate position between the use configuration and the storage configuration;

FIG. 3C is a simplified sectional side elevation view showing the folding table from FIG. 3A in the storage configuration; and

FIG. 4 is a rear elevation view of the folding table in the use configuration.

DETAILED DESCRIPTION

A folding table with a two position leg lock is described herein and illustrated in the accompanying figures. Aspects of the folding table include a pair of regular, non- foldable legs and a pair of foldable legs that move between a use configuration and a storage configuration. The foldable legs incorporate a two position lock mechanism that selectively allows the legs to be locked in either the use configuration where the legs cooperatively support the table top or the storage configuration where the legs are positioned parallel to the table top. The table top includes a notched lip that allows the legs to lie substantially flush against the bottom surface of the table top.

Figure 1 is a perspective view of one embodiment of the folding table in a use configuration. The folding table 100 *includes a table top 102, a pair of regular (i.e., non-foldable) legs 104, and a pair of foldable legs 106. Each foldable leg 106 includes a base leg segment 108 and a leg extension 110. Each fixed (i.e., non-folding) leg 104, base leg segment 108, and leg extension 110 has an upper end 112 and a lower end 114. The folding table described herein is suitable for use in variety of folding table implementations, including, without limitation, folding cocktail tables where the length of the legs exceeds the diameter or other relevant dimension the table top 102.*

In the embodiment depicted in Figure I, the folding table 100 is shown in the use configuration. The regular legs 104 and the foldable legs 106 are configured to cooperatively support the table top 102 in a substantially horizontal orientation when in the use configuration. Generally, the upper ends 112 of the regular legs 104 and the leg extensions 110 are connected to the table top 102, either directly or indirectly. The lower ends 114 of the regular legs 104 and base leg segments 108 generally engage the ground or other supporting surface when the folding table 100 is in the use configuration.

Each of the regular legs 104 is operatively connected to one of base leg segments 108 of the foldable legs 106 by main connectors 116 aligned on a first common pivot axis. The main connectors 116 are generally located centrally along the regular legs 104. The exact placement of the main connectors 116 varies depending upon the height of the folding table 100 and the spacing between the upper ends 112 of the regular legs 104 and the foldable legs 106. In operation, the regular legs 104 and foldable legs 106 operate as double levers with the main connectors 116 operating as the fulcrums about which the interconnected legs pivot in a scissor-like manner.

Each base leg segment 108 of the foldable legs 106 is operatively connected to one of the leg extensions 110 by foldable leg connectors 118 generally aligned on a second common pivot axis. The foldable leg connectors 118 are generally located proximate to the upper ends 112 of the base leg segments 108 and proximate to the lower ends 114 of the leg extensions

110. In other words, the foldable leg connectors 118 are to vary the overall length of the foldable legs 106 depending upon the relative orientation of the leg extensions 110 to the base leg segments 108. When in the use configuration, the foldable legs 106 are fully extended (i.e., the lower ends 114 of the base leg segments 108 and the leg extensions 110 are oriented in the same direction), and the combined length of the base leg segment 108 from the lower end 114 to the foldable leg connector 118 and the leg extension 110 from the upper end 112 to the connector is substantially equal to the length of the fixed leg 104.

In operation, the base leg segments 108 and the extensions 110 pivot about the connectors 118 moving from the use configuration where lower ends 114 of the base leg segments 108 point in the opposite direction from the upper ends 112 of the leg extensions 110 to a storage configuration where the lower ends 114 of the base leg segments 108 point in the same direction as the upper ends 112 of the leg extensions 110. A lock mechanism 122 allows the foldable legs 106 and the extensions 110 to be selectively fixed in the use configuration or the storage configuration. In some embodiments, each of the fixed legs 104, the base leg segments 108, and the leg extensions 110 on one side of the folding table 100 move independently from those on the other side of the folding table 100. In other embodiments, such as the illustrated embodiment, one or more optional cross members 120 connect the regular legs

104, base leg segments 108, and leg extensions 110. When included, the cross members 120 provide structural stability by fixing the positions of the individual regular legs 104, base leg segments 108, and leg extensions 110 relative to each other. More specifically, the cross members 120 maintain the distance between the individual regular legs 104, base leg segments 108, and leg extensions 110 to facilitate folding and unfolding the table 100 by moving the paired regular legs 104, base leg segments 108, and leg extensions 110 together, which reduces binding on the connectors 116, 118. The cross members 120 may also offer ancillary functionality. For example, depending upon position, the cross members 120 may serve as handles for repositioning the legs or carrying the table 100 or footrests. In the illustrated embodiment, two techniques for implementing the cross members 120 are shown. The cross member 120 connecting the leg extensions 110 is illustrated as forming a continuous structure with a U-shape, while the cross members 120 connecting the regular legs 104 and the base leg segments 108, respectively, are separate pieces. The number and positions of the cross members can be varied for reasons such as, but not limited to, aesthetics, structural integrity, and ancillary functionality.

In various embodiments, the folding table 100 includes a pair of notches 124 defined by the lip 126 of the table top 102. The notches 124 allow the legs 104, 106 to lie substantially flush with the bottom of the *lip 126 and provide a generally flat profile while in the storage configuration. The lip 126 optionally extends below the attachment points where the legs connect to the table top and provides support to keep the legs and attachment points elevated to reduce the risk of damage (e.g., bending) when the bottom of the folding table rests on a supporting surface. The lip 126 is optionally sized to substantially match or exceed the thickness of the legs 104, 106 to provide a level base when the folding table 100 is in the storage configuration, which facilitates stacking of the folding tables.*

Figure 2 is a bottom plan view of one embodiment of the folding table 100 in a storage configuration. The underside of the table top 102 includes attachment points 202 where the upper ends 112 of the regular legs 104 and the leg extensions 110 are pivotally secured to the table top 102. Various types of attachment points may be used. In the illustrated embodiment, two different types of attachment points 202 are implemented. The attachment points 202 used with the regular legs 104 are brackets 202a that hold a pivot arm (e.g., a cylindrical tube) 204 that connects the upper ends 112 of the regular legs 104 and defines the pivot axis. The brackets 202a provide support and allow the pivot arm 204 to rotate. The attachment points 202 used with the leg extensions 110 are tabs 202b with each tab 202b supporting a pivot pin that connects to the upper end of one of the leg extensions 110. In some embodiments, the attachment points 202 are located on a frame 206 that is attached to and supports the table top 102. In other embodiments, the attachment points 202 are connected directed to the table top 102.

In embodiments incorporating a frame 206, the table top 102 is optional. This allows the folding table described herein to be implemented as folding table frame with a table top 102 to be added at a later time. For reference, the term upper support member broadly encompasses a table top, a frame, or combination thereof.

When in the storage configuration, the regular legs 104 and the foldable legs 106 lie in the same plane. However, the points of origin (i.e., the attachment points 202) for the regular legs 104 and the foldable *legs 106 are offset. Because the regular legs 104 and the foldable legs 106 are connected at a fixed location (i.e., main connectors 116), it becomes necessary to compensate for the offset between the points of origin in order place the regular legs 104 and the foldable legs 106 into the storage configuration. By folding the foldable legs 106 at the foldable leg connector 118 such that the lower ends 114 of the base leg segments 108 and the leg extensions 110 are oriented in the opposite directions, the effective length of the foldable legs 106 is reduced to compensate for the offset.*

In the illustrated embodiment, the legs members 108 have different lengths. The additional length of the longer base leg segment 108 is used to implement the lock mechanism 122. However, it is not necessary for the base leg segments 108 to have different lengths. An example of a suitable lock mechanism 122 is a lock pin main connector extending from one of the leg extensions 110. The lock pin 208 is biased to normally extend beyond the outside edge of the leg extension 110 toward the base leg segment 108. For example, a captured spring may bias the lock pin 208 toward the extended position. An actuator or handle 210, such as the depicted ring, allows an operator to apply a force opposing the bias to retract the lock pin thereby disengaging the lock mechanism 122. In the illustrated embodiment, the lock pin 208 is captured by the leg extension 110 to minimize the risk of loss. Further, a permanently mounted locking mechanism 122 is not a requirement and a free lock pin may be used. If desired, the free lock pin may be attached by a cable to minimize the risk of loss. Other lock mechanisms, such as, detents and other mechanisms for preventing relative movement of two connected members may be used.

Further, the illustrated embodiment shows the regular legs 104 positioned on the outside of the foldable legs 106 and the leg extensions 110 positioned to the inside of the base leg segments 108. Aspects of the folding table 100 are described herein using the depicted leg arrangement to provide a frame of reference. However, the folding table 100 may be suitably implemented using other leg arrangements and, as such, any directional references, such as inward or outward, inside or outside, and the like should not be read as limiting the folding table 100 to the depicted implementation.

Figures 3A-C are simplified sectional side elevation views, taken along line 3-3 of Figure 2, showing the folding table in various positions and aspects of the lock mechanism 122. The arrow B on the base leg segment 108 and arrow E the leg extension 110 point to the upper ends 112 and provide an visual indication of the relative orientations of the segments of the foldable leg 106 in the use configuration (FIG. 3A), an exemplary intermediate position between the use configuration and the storage configuration (FIG. 3B), and the storage configuration (FIG. 3C).

As shown in Figure 3 A, the lock mechanism 122 includes a lock pin 208 extending from one of the leg extensions 110. A use receptacle 304 and a storage receptacle 306 defined by the connected base leg segment 108, which are normally hidden by the leg extension 110 while in the use and storage configurations (and various positions in between), are illustrated in phantom.

The lock pin 208 is offset from the foldable leg connector 118 by a selected distance in the direction of the lower end 114 of the leg extension 110. The use receptacle 304 is offset from the foldable leg connector 118 by a selected distance in the direction of the lower end 114 of the leg extension 110. The storage receptacle 306 is offset from the foldable leg connector 118 by substantially the same distance in the direction of the upper end 112 of the leg extension 110. In other words, the lock pin 208 and the receptacles 304, 306 lie on the circumference of a circle with a radius, r, and centered on the foldable leg connector 118. Thus, when in the use configuration, the lock pin 208 and the use receptacle 304 are aligned, and, when in the use configuration, the lock pin 208 and the storage receptacle 306 are aligned. It will be appreciated that some variation of the distances is permissible within the alignment tolerances of the lock pin 208 and the receptacles 304, 306.

The receptacles 304, 306 are configured to receive the lock pin 208 in operative engagement. When the lock pin 208 is aligned with and inserted into one of the receptacles 304, 306, the position of the connected base leg segment 108 becomes locked relative to the leg extension 110. Locking the foldable leg 106 prevents the regular legs 104 and foldable legs 106 from moving.

In Figure 3A, the lock pin 208 is operatively engaged with the use receptacle thereby securing the folding table 100 in the use configuration. In the use configuration, the base leg segment 108 and the leg extension 110 are parallel and oriented in the same direction to provide the maximum length for the foldable leg 106, which is the same length as the fixed leg 104.

In Figure 3B, the lock pin 208 is extended but not engaged and may need to be retracted to allow the foldable leg to be placed into the use or storage configuration, as desired.

In Figure 3C, the lock pin 208 is operatively engaged with the storage receptacle 306 thereby securing the folding table 100 in the storage configuration. The legs are oriented to 104, 106 point away from the fixed leg attachment point 302a. In the storage configuration, the base leg segment 108 and the leg extension 110 are parallel but oriented in opposite directions to provide the minimum length for the foldable leg 106. The minimum length of the foldable leg 106 combined with the distance between the fixed leg attachment point 302a and the foldable leg attachment point 302b is the same as the length of the fixed leg 104. In this view, the fixed leg 104 is behind the foldable leg 106 and is not visible.

Figure 4 is a rear elevation view of the folding table. In addition to providing another perspective of various aspects of the folding table 100 previously discussed herein, the illustrated embodiment includes a set of tab stops 402 attached to the rear of the base leg segments 108. The tab stops 402 extend inward toward the leg extensions 110. As the foldable leg 106 is unfolded into the use configuration and the base leg segments 108 align with the leg extensions 110, the tab stops 402 contact the rear surface of the leg extensions 110 and prevent further movement. This protects the foldable leg

106 from rotating beyond the position of the use configuration during deployment.

The various features and aspects described in reference to the particular embodiments of the invention described herein are intended to be considered independent and optional. The depiction of any particular embodiment containing a combination of one or more features or aspects is not intended to require all such features or aspects to be incorporated into all embodiments of the invention. The disclosure should be read to encompass intermediate embodiments omitting one or more features or aspects disclosed as a combination in a particular embodiment and alternate embodiments composed of selected features or aspects from one or more disclosed embodiments even though all such combinations or alternative embodiments were not expressly enumerated. By way of example in the present application, any particular embodiment or implementation of the folding table 100 may selectively include or omit independent and optional features, such as and without limitation, the table top 102, the cross members 120, the notches 124, the lip 126, the frame 206, and the tab stops 402.

The foregoing description of embodiments for this invention has been presented for purposes of illustration and description. It is not intended to be exhaustive or to limit the invention to the precise form disclosed. Obvious modifications or variations are possible in light of the above teachings. The *embodiments are chosen and described in an effort to provide illustrations of the principles of the invention and its practical application, and to thereby enable one of ordinary skill in the art to utilize the invention in various embodiments and with various modifications as are suited to the particular use contemplated. All such modifications and variations are within the scope of the invention as determined by the appended claims when interpreted in accordance with the breadth to which they are fairly, legally, and equitably entitled.*

Claims

Hide Dependent

CLAIMS What is claimed is:

1. A folding table having a storage configuration and a use configuration, the folding table comprising: an upper support member configured to be substantially horizontal when in the use configuration; a set of regular legs, each fixed leg having an upper end and a lower end, the upper end of each fixed leg pivotally connected to the upper support member; a set of foldable legs, each foldable leg having a base leg segment and a leg extension, each base leg segment and each leg extension having an upper end and a lower end, the upper end of each leg extension pivotally connected to the upper support member, the upper end of each base leg segment pivotally connected to the leg extension at a first pivot axis, each base leg segment pivotally connected to one of the regular legs at a second pivot axis; a set of lock receptacles defined by the set of foldable legs, the set of lock receptacles comprising a use receptacle positioned on one side of the first pivot axis and a storage receptacle positioned on the opposite side of the first pivot axis, the use receptacle and the storage receptacle being offset from the first pivot axis by a selected distance; and a lock pin for selectively engaging one of the use receptacle and the storage receptacle to selectively lock the leg extension to the first base segment in the use configuration and the storage configuration and to prevent movement of the foldable legs relative to the regular legs.

2. The folding table of claim 1 wherein the second pivot axis is located in a middle area of the regular legs allowing the regular legs and the foldable legs to move in scissor-like manner.

3. The folding table of claim 1 wherein the upper support member is a table top or a frame configured to support a table top.

4. The folding table of claim 3 wherein the regular legs are longer than the widest dimension of the table top.

5. The folding table of claim 3 wherein the table top comprises a perimetrical lip projecting from the table top, the lip defining at least one notch receiving the regular legs and the foldable legs when in the storage configuration.

6. The folding table of claim 1 wherein the regular legs and the foldable legs move between the use configuration wherein the base leg segments the leg extensions are parallel with the upper ends pointing in the same direction and the storage configuration wherein the base leg segments and the leg extensions are parallel to the upper support member with the upper ends pointing in opposite directions.

7. The folding table of claim 1 further comprising at least one cross member connected between at least one pair of the regular legs, the base leg segments, and the leg extensions.

8. The folding table of claim 1 further comprising a cross member connecting the lower ends of the leg extensions.

9. The folding table of claim 1 further comprising a set of tabs extending laterally from one of the leg extensions or the base leg segments, the tabs engaging the other of the leg extensions or the base leg segments when moved to the use configuration and blocking movement of the leg extensions past the use configuration.

10. The folding table of claim 1 wherein:

the set of lock receptacles is defined by a first one of the base leg segments, the use receptacle positioned between the first pivot axis and the second pivot axis, the storage receptacle positioned between the first pivot axis and the upper end of the first base leg segments; and the lock pin is carried by the leg extension connected to the first base leg segment.

11. The folding table of claim 1 wherein:
the set of lock receptacles is defined by a first one of the leg extensions, the use receptacle positioned between the first pivot axis and the lower end of the leg extension, the storage receptacle positioned between the first pivot axis and the upper end of the first leg extension; and

the lock pin is carried by a first one of the base leg segments connected to the first leg extension.

12. The folding table of claim 1 wherein the lock pin is normally biased to extend in the direction of the base leg segment or the leg extension which defines the set of lock receptacles.

13. The folding table of claim 1 wherein the lock pin is selectively retractable to

disengage the lock pin from the use receptacle or the storage receptacle allowing the base leg segments and the leg extensions to pivot relative to one another and the regular legs and the foldable legs to pivot relative to one another.

14. The folding table of claim 1 wherein the first base leg segment is longer than the other base leg segment.

15. A folding table having a storage configuration and a use configuration, the folding table comprising:

a table top comprising a top surface and a perimetrical lip, the perimetrical lip defining at least one notch; a set of regular legs, each fixed leg having an upper end and a lower end, the upper end of each fixed leg pivotally connected to the table top, the set of regular legs being substantially parallel to and extending beyond the table top through the at least one notch when in the storage configuration;

a set of foldable legs, each foldable leg having a base leg segment and a leg extension, each base leg segment and each leg extension having an upper end and a lower end, the upper end of each leg extension pivotally connected to the table top, the upper end of each base leg segment pivotally connected to the leg extension at a first pivot axis, each base leg segment pivotally connected to one of the regular legs at a second pivot axis; and a lock mechanism operable to secure the position of the regular legs relative to the foldable legs when in the use configuration and in the storage configuration.

16. The folding table of claim 15 wherein the lock mechanism comprises:

a first opening defined by a first member of one of the foldable legs, the first opening located at a selected distance from the first pivot axis in a first direction, the first member being either the base leg segment or the leg extension; a second opening defined by the first member, the second opening located at the selected distance from the first pivot axis in a second direction opposite to the first direction; and a lock pin carried by a second member, the second member being the other member of the foldable leg, the lock pin located at the selected distance from the first pivot axis toward the upper end of the second member, the lock pin selectively engaging one of the first opening and the second opening when the first member and second member are positioned in parallel to prevent movement of the first member relative to the second member.

17. The folding table of claim 16 wherein the lock pin is selectively retractable to disengage the lock pin from the use receptacle or the storage receptacle allowing the base leg segments and the leg extensions to pivot relative to one another and the regular legs and the foldable legs to pivot relative to one another.

18. The folding table of claim 15 wherein the regular legs and the foldable legs move between the use configuration

wherein the base leg segments the leg extensions are parallel with the upper ends pointing in the same direction and the storage configuration wherein the base leg segments and the leg extensions are parallel to the upper support member with the upper ends pointing in opposite directions.

19. The folding table of claim 15 further comprising a set of tabs extending laterally from one of the leg extensions or the base leg segments, the tabs engaging the other of the leg extensions or the base leg segments when moved to the use configuration and blocking movement of the leg extensions past the use configuration.

20. A folding table having a storage configuration and a use configuration, the folding table comprising:

a table top comprising a top surface and a perimetrical lip, the perimetrical lip defining a set of notches, the table top having a height and a width; a set of regular legs, each fixed leg having an upper end and a lower end, the upper end of each fixed leg pivotally connected to the table top, the regular legs having a length greater than the height and width of the table top, each fixed leg being substantially parallel to the table top and resting in one of the notches when in the storage configuration; a set of foldable legs, each foldable leg having a base leg segment and a leg extension, each base leg segment and each leg extension having an upper end and a lower end, the upper end of each leg extension pivotally connected to the table top, the upper end of each base leg segment pivotally connected to the leg extension at a first pivot axis, each base leg segment pivotally connected to one of the regular legs at a second pivot axis, the foldable legs movable between

the use configuration wherein the base leg segments and the leg extensions are parallel to each other and the upper ends of the base leg segments and the leg extensions are pointing in the same direction, and the storage configuration wherein the base leg segments and the leg extensions are parallel to the table top and the upper ends of the base leg segments and the leg extensions are *pointing in opposite directions; a first opening and a second opening defined by one of a first base leg segment or a first leg extension, the first opening located at a selected distance from the first pivot axis in a first direction, the second opening located at the selected distance from the first pivot axis in a second direction opposite to the first direction; and a lock pin carried by the other of the first base leg segment or the first leg extension, the lock pin located at the selected distance from the first pivot axis toward the upper end of the second member, the lock pin selectively engaging one of the first opening and the second opening when the first member and second member are positioned in parallel to prevent movement of the first base leg segment relative to the first leg extension.*

Once the State of the Art Report (SOAR) was made for this patent, the result indicated that the following similar previous patents existed:

The result of SOAR indicated the following patents cited with an X, which means that the current patent application coincides with one or more claims, therefore it lacks novelty and/or inventive activity:

- US10330245B2 2019-06-25 Metrology grade light weight tripod

- US9950728B2 2018-04-24 Collapsible table

- TW449637B 2001-08-11 Folding stage

- *KR200479669Y1   2016-02-23   Device for preventing falling down of ladder*

- *US20160008070A1   2016-01-14
        Expandable and foldable mayo stand*

- *JP2012514523A   2012-06-28   Soccer goal*

- *US11478075B2   2022-10-25   Foldable shelving*

- *EP3405070B12020-11-18   Folding   table with two-position leg lock*

- *CN102317564B   2015-09-30   For object support unit and comprise the device of this support unit*

- *JP2012521847A   2012-09-20   Infant chair with foldable legs*

- *KR20220058539A   2022-05-09   folding height adjustable table*

- CN110430781B   2022-06-14   Folding piano support capable of mutually stretching

- CA3049893C 2021-05-25   Articulated support bracket

- US20180055213A1   2018-03-01   Table

- JPH08254037A   1996-10-01   Folding supporter such as deck

- JPH0768088A   1995-03-14   Improved bendable clothesline

- US10130167B1   2018-11-20   Foldable table

- US6382716B1   2002-05-07   Folding chair with safety guard

- US8302540B1   2012-11-06 Extendable folding table

- JP2010279627A   2010-12-16   Stick also serving as chair

- US11617448B2   2023-04-04   Bed frame

- EP3671000A1   2020-06-24   A compact stand for a television camera

- US9622569B2   2017-04-18   Compact-stand, folding table

- EP3225130B12018-12-19   Foldable furniture with a locking hinge assembly

- KR101695785B1   2017-01-23   Foldable Music Stand

Source: Google Patents

The date of the previous patents does not matter since a previous patent, regardless of whether it is still in force or not, nullifies the novelty or the inventive step because it has already been disclosed.

On the other hand, simply by analyzing the titles of the previous patents, you will have deduced that some of those mentioned in said report are inventions very different to a "Folding table with two-position leg lock" , but it doesn't matter! As you will have already learned by reading this book; if some earlier invention uses a technique described in your patent, even if that technique is used for another purpose, the result could be that your patent is not considered to have an inventive step because it can be deduced from what already exists patented or from what already exists in the public domain.

I would like to express my special gratitude to Catherine M. Anner for her dedication and enthusiasm in the translation of this book

www.ingramcontent.com/pod-product-compliance
Lightning Source LLC
Chambersburg PA
CBHW072337290526
45794CB00002B/906